The Understanding

Your Suicide Grief

Support Group Guide

Also by Alan Wolfelt

The Handbook for Companioning the Mourner:
Eleven Essential Principles

Healing a Friend's Grieving Heart:
100 Practical Ideas for Helping Someone
You Love Through Loss

Healing Your Traumatized Heart: 100 Practical Ideas After
Someone You Love Dies a Sudden, Violent Death

Living in the Shadow of the Ghosts of Grief:
Step Into the Light

Understanding Your Suicide Grief: Ten Essential
Touchstones for Finding Hope and Healing Your Heart

The Understanding Your Suicide Grief Journal:
Exploring the Ten Essential Touchstones

The Wilderness of Suicide Grief: Finding Your Way

Companion
P R E S S

Companion Press is dedicated to the education and support
of both the bereaved and bereavement caregivers. We believe
that those who companion the bereaved by walking with them
as they journey in grief have a wondrous opportunity: to help
others embrace and grow through grief—and to lead fuller, more
deeply-lived lives themselves because of this important ministry.

For a complete catalog and ordering information, write or call:

Companion Press
The Center for Loss and Life Transition
3735 Broken Bow Road
Fort Collins, Colorado 80526
(970) 226-6050
DrWolfelt@centerforloss.com
www.centerforloss.com

The Understanding Your Suicide Grief
Support Group Guide

Meeting Plans for Facilitators

Alan D. Wolfelt, Ph.D.

Companion
PRESS

Fort Collins, Colorado
An imprint of the Center for Loss and Life Transition

Companion Press is an imprint of the Center for Loss and Life Transition, 3735 Broken Bow Road, Fort Collins, Colorado 80526.

Printed in the United States of America.

18 17 16 15 14 13 12 11 10 09   5 4 3 2 1

ISBN: 978-1879651-60-9

Contents

The Understanding Your Suicide Grief

Support Group Guide:
Meeting Plans for Facilitators

Author's note: This book provides guidance and plans for a 12-session support group based on Understanding Your Suicide Grief. *If you are an experienced grief support group leader, this book provides you with easy-to-use plans for both you and the group participants to follow throughout the 12 weeks. If you are a layperson who would like to start a support group but have no support group experience or formal psychology training, I encourage you to follow through on your instinct to help both yourself and others. You <u>can</u> start a support group! I would strongly recommend, however, that you find an experienced support group leader or grief counselor to help you run the meetings. What's more, if you personally are to be one of the group's co-leaders, you should be in a place in your own grief journey where you have emerged from the wilderness and have successfully integrated the death into your life. If you are too early in your own grief journey, you are probably not ready yet to be an effective group facilitator.*

An excellent tool to assist in the grief process is participating in a support group. Grief support groups bring people together in the common bond of experience.

Before starting a suicide support group of your own, do some checking around in your community. Someone nearby may already be successfully facilitating a suicide support group, and you may simply be able to enroll in one of the next sessions. If you do decide to start a support group, first do some planning. We have all heard that the three keys in real estate are location, location, location. Well, the three keys to a successful grief support group are planning, planning, planning.

Preferably, the group should include two leaders, which will enable them to plan and debrief meetings together. In a mixed-gender group, it is usually helpful to have one male and one female leader. The leaders could be either professional caregivers sensitive to the model outlined in this book, or laypersons who have been through the wilderness of suicide grief and gone on to experience reconciliation. Laypeople may find it helpful to find a consultant/advisor familiar with group process and the dynamics of grief transition to support and help them. Because of the sensitive nature of suicide grief in particular, assembling an advisory board of counseling and related professionals is also a prudent idea.

Skilled leadership will be a major determinant of the success of your support group. So, if you are interested in starting a group based on this book, I urge you to find skilled people for the leadership roles. Effective group leaders are well-prepared. They plan each meeting much in the same way teachers prepare lesson plans: with a flexible structure and a purposeful sequencing of activities. In other words, they don't just "wing it."

Through the years I have found that groups that are closed-ended (meaning that the group will meet for a specific, finite number of weeks) and education-based (meaning there are elements of learning about aspects of the suicide grief journey) but that also include open discussion (meaning that any education period is followed by a dedicated time for open discussion and

2

exploration) work very well. I then encourage people to graduate to more open-ended groups (meaning group members come and go depending on their needs, and there is usually less-structured educational content). The primary reason that I strongly suggest this is that so many people come to the grief experience needing some basic information (such as misconceptions about suicide grief, the unique influences on their experience, the central needs of mourning, etc.) to help them on their way into and through the wilderness.

Following is a set of twelve meeting plans that interface with *Understanding Your Suicide Grief* and the companion journal. These meeting plans are only intended as suggested guidelines. Be creative and consider creating some of your own activities that you think may better serve the needs of your unique group.

My experience suggests that the format that follows encourages the members to participate and provides them a comfortable structure that promotes open exploration and discussion. (Of course, my hope is that it also helps you as a leader!)

Please note that during the first meeting, you should be prepared to pass out copies of *Understanding Your Suicide Grief* and the companion journal, *The Understanding Your Suicide Grief Journal*, to all participants. If you order all of the books from my Center for Loss and Life Transition, you will receive a discounted price, which you can then pass along to the group members (call 970-226-6050 or visit www.centerforloss.com to order).

Between each session, group members will be asked to read a chapter from the main book and complete the corresponding journal chapter. This support group model works best if participants do indeed take the time and energy to fill out their journals as completely as possible. Not only does journaling provide them with a healthy way to encounter and express their grief, it produces a record of their support group experience.

But not everyone is a journaler. Don't be surprised if at least one or two of your group members are reluctant to journal—perhaps

3

even refusing to complete this part of the homework each week. You know what they say: You can lead a participant to the guided questions, but you can't make him write down the answers. So, if one or more of your group members won't journal, that's okay. Just encourage them to read the text and at least read through and consider the journal questions. And try not to allow the non-journaler's laxity to influence the rest of the group; if others see that journaling is "optional," they may be inclined to let it slip as well. Keep reminding your group members of the value of the journaling process.

Support group meeting plan—Session One
Introduction to the Group

Introduction/Welcome

Welcome the participants to the meeting and provide a brief orientation to the purpose of the support group. The introduction and orientation could include comments such as the following (if you are using a co-leader, as I hope you are, you will of course say "we" instead of "I"):

Thanks so much for coming to this support group. We welcome each and every one of you. As you know, this group will be a combined education-support group. We will be using the books *Understanding Your Suicide Grief* and *The Understanding Your Suicide Grief Journal*. As group leaders, we believe you will find these resources to be supportive and bring you hope.

Each of our meetings will last 90 minutes; we will meet every week for twelve weeks. The first half of the meeting will be a discussion based on some content from the books. The second half of each meeting will be left open for group sharing.

At tonight's meeting, we will begin to get to know each other, distribute the books, and go over our group ground rules. Before we get started, does anyone have any questions or concerns? Again, we thank each of you for being here tonight.

Next, the leader (that's you!) will distribute a printed list of the group ground rules you have created prior to the first meeting. The group will then review the ground rules and ask questions or share concerns. Your group may wish to make changes or additions to this list.

Sample Suicide Grief Support Group Ground Rules

1. Each person's grief is unique. While you may share some commonalities in your experiences, no two of you are exactly alike. Consequently, respect and accept both what you have in common with others and what is unique to each of you.
2. Grief is not a disease, and no "quick-fix" exists for what you are feeling. Don't set a specific timetable for how long it should take you or others to heal.
3. Feel free to talk about your grief. However, if someone in the group decides to listen without sharing, please respect his or her preference.
4. There is a difference between actively listening to what another person is saying and expressing your own grief. Make every effort not to interrupt when someone else is speaking.
5. Thoughts, feelings, and experiences shared in this group will stay in this group. Respect others' right to confidentiality. Do not use names of fellow participants in discussions outside the group.
6. Allow each person equal time to express himself or herself so a few people don't monopolize the group's time.
7. Attend each group meeting and be on time. If you decide to leave the group before this series of meetings is completed, be willing to discuss your decision with the group.
8. Avoid "advice giving" unless it is specifically requested by a group member. If advice is not solicited, don't give it. If a group member poses a question, share ideas that helped you if you experienced a similar situation. Remember that this group is for support, not therapy.
9. Recognize that thoughts and feelings are neither right nor wrong. Enter into the thoughts and feelings of other group members without trying to change them
10. Create an atmosphere of willing, invited sharing. If you feel pressured to talk but don't want to, say so. Your right to quiet contemplation will be respected by the group.

Facilitate Initial Introductions of Group Members

Following a review and discussion of the ground rules, you as facilitator can model introducing yourself. If you have suffered a suicide death in your own life, you can share a little about your experience and why you are leading this support group. Then you can invite others to do the same. Obviously, part of your role is to bring sensitivity and encouragement to the group members.

To make it safe for the participants to introduce themselves, be sure to provide topics for the introductions. For example: "To help us start to get to know each other, please tell us your name, a little about the suicide in your life, and what your hopes from being in this group are. If each of us takes four or five minutes to do this, it will be very helpful. Again, thanks for your willingness to be here." Please note: You are purposefully not having them go into great detail about the circumstances of the deaths at this point. You are trying to gently enter into the process and helping them begin to feel safe with each other, the group experience, and you. Trust in the process, and don't panic when some members take more time than others. This naturally occurs as more people speak and trust begins to be established. Some members may talk more initially out of anxiety, while others will appear withdrawn and may even have to pass.

Again, trust in the process. If a member feels the need to pause for a while, the group will understand. Tears need not be forced, but certainly will be accepted if they occur. If necessary, you may gently remind the group not to interrupt with questions when members are first introducing themselves.

At this first meeting, the sharing process is an important initial step in creating a supportive, healing group experience. As people begin to share themselves, a powerful bonding often begins. Go slowly. As I always say, "There are no rewards for speed." Listen, learn, and heal.

Distribute Resources

At the conclusion of the group introductions, you will distribute copies of the two books (*Understanding Your Suicide Grief* and *The Understanding Your Suicide Grief Journal*) to each person. Explain to members that the first book is for reading and the journal is for expressing their thoughts and feelings about what they read. Explain that the books introduce the concept of the ten Touchstones that are essential physical, emotional, cognitive, social, and spiritual actions for you to take if your goal is to heal from your grief experience and find continued meaning in life.

Discuss Homework

Everyone is asked to read the Introduction to both books and Touchstone One in *Understanding Your Suicide Grief* before the next meeting. Invite and encourage the members to complete the journal for these sections (through p. 16). Obviously, group members should be asked to come prepared to discuss the material and their reactions to what they have both read and written. Members also should be asked not to read ahead in the books; reading the primary book and completing the journal will be a shared group experience.

Again, thank everyone for being a vital part of this group and let them know you look forward to seeing them next week.

Session One Notes

_____

_____

_____

_____

_____

_____

_____

_____

_____

Support group meeting plan—Session Two

Introduction to the Texts and Touchstone One

This meeting is when you begin to model how nicely it works to reflect on the content of *Understanding Your Suicide Grief* in the first half of your meeting and then shift to more open-ended discussion in the second half. Of course, all the time you are modeling good leadership skills, being sure to include everyone in ways that make them feel welcomed and included.

You will find that there are too many questions in the journal section each week to go through them one by one during the meeting. Instead, I suggest you pick out three or four that your unique group might be responsive to exploring and lead a discussion about them. There will be time in the second half of the meeting for group members to bring up whatever they want to talk about, which might include some of the journal questions not covered in the first half of the meeting. Use the remaining questions to encourage open exploration, discussion, and group sharing. Stay flexible and responsive to your group.

Potential topics (from the journal) for discussion from the Introduction and Welcome to the book:

You might initially ask some very open-ended questions such as: "As you read the Introduction to *Understanding Your Suicide Grief*, what thoughts and feelings came to mind for you? Does the concept of "Touchstones" or "trail markers" make sense to you? What did you think of Dr. Wolfelt's thought that we need to "surrender" to this experience? What did you think of the discussions of hope, heart, and courage? What was your response from just reading the Introduction?"

Key topics (from the journal) for discussion:

* *Dosing your pain*
  Suicide grief is typically profoundly painful and

overwhelming. What have group members learned about the need to "dose" their pain?

• *Setting your intention to heal*
You might consider asking each group member in turn to read what he or she has written in response to the journal question on p.12. This can be a powerful motivational discussion that sets the tone for the healing to come.

• *Shock versus denial*
Invite group members to share their experiences with feelings of shock and denial. What types of denial have some of the members experienced or witnessed in others they know? How are they gently and in doses working to soften any long-term denial?

• *Grief is not a disease*
Discuss the ways in which group members have taken (and are taking) steps to help themselves begin to heal.

Use your leadership qualities and skills to facilitate the discussions each and every week. Approximately the second half of this and every following session should be used for open-ended discussion. However, keep in mind that each and every group will have its own unique tone and dynamic. Allow each meeting to flow naturally.

Homework

For the next meeting, each participant should be asked to read Touchstone Two—Dispel the Misconceptions About Suicide and Grief and Mourning (pp. 35-52) and complete the companion journal section (pp. 17-32).

Session Two Notes

_____

_____

_____

_____

Support group meeting plan—Session Three

Touchstone Two—Dispel the Misconceptions About Suicide Grief and Mourning

After initial warm-up, I suggest that you lead an open discussion of the Misconceptions about Grief outlined in Touchstone Two. There is enough content here that discussion usually comes easily to members. They often like to give examples of how they have experienced these misconceptions in their own journeys.

Again, use the questions outlined in the journal to encourage open exploration, discussion, and group sharing. This journal chapter has many, many questions—too many to cover during group. Pick just a few and concentrate on those, then if there's time, continue discussion with more of the questions.

Key topics (from the journal) for discussion:

- *The difference between grief and mourning*
  On a chalkboard or flipchart, make two columns. Title one "Grief" and the other "Mourning." The purpose here is to make sure that group members understand the difference between the two, and to help them focus on not only grieving the death, but mourning the death. Get examples of grief and mourning and write them in the appropriate column. (For example, sadness would go under grief; crying would go under mourning.)

- *All suicide survivors feel guilty*
  Facilitate a discussion about suicide and guilt. Be certain that you are not prescribing to group members that they SHOULD feel guilty. The purpose of this discussion is to explore any potential feelings of guilt that *might* exist as well as the tendency for others to assume that suicide survivors feel guilty. Discuss the difference between blame and responsibility.

- *Explore the various misconceptions*
  Go right down through the list of the different misconceptions and see what comes up in discussion.

Several of the misconceptions will usually spark quite a bit of discussion and further bond your group.

Remember—approximately the second half of this session can be used for open-ended discussion.

Homework

For the next meeting, each participant should be asked to read Touchstone Three—Explore the Uniqueness of Your Suicide Grief (pp. 53-68) and complete the companion journal section (pp. 33-56).

Session Three Notes

Support group meeting plan—Session Four

Touchstone Three—Embrace the Uniqueness of Your Suicide Grief

After initial warm-up, I suggest that you lead a discussion of the unique influences on grief outlined in Touchstone Three. On a chalkboard or flipchart, write the ten "Whys" listed in this chapter. (You might also include one additional heading called "Other;" this creates a place for you to write down group responses that don't fit in one of the ten "Whys.") Just by looking at the chalkboard, the group can then easily recall the ten influences and explore the various questions related to them in their journals.

Time will probably not allow participants to explore each question under each "Why," so use your judgment in processing them. Depending on your group size, you may want to break into two groups. Your skills in group process are part of the art of leading this group and making decisions about how to best lead each meeting.

Key topics (from the journal) for discussion:

• *The circumstance of the suicide (Why #1)*
  This can be a difficult topic for participants. But it's helpful to talk about it and get support from fellow group members. Obviously, you will model active listening and support the unfolding process. People may feel it helpful to simply read some of what they have written about this in their journals.

• *Your relationship with the person who completed suicide (Why #2)*
  Referring to the prompts in the journal (pp. 34-37), ask participants to share their thoughts or stories about their unique relationships with the person who died.

Obviously, you can facilitate discussion around the additional "Whys" and invite members to brainstorm other "Whys" as well. Again, the second half of the session can be used for open-ended discussion.

Homework

For the next meeting, each participant should be asked to read Touchstone Four – Explore Your Feelings of Loss (pp. 69-112) and complete the companion journal section (pp. 57-80).

Session Four Notes

_____

_____

_____

_____

_____

_____

_____

_____

_____

_____

_____

_____

_____

_____

_____

_____

_____

_____

_____

_____

_____

_____

_____

_____

_____

_____

_____

_____

_____

_____

_____

_____

Support group meeting plan—Session Five

Touchstone Four—Explore Your Feelings of Loss

This meeting is about all the various feelings participants might have as part of the grief experience. As you know, these feelings can be all over the map. Some people feel angry, some feel numb, some feel ashamed. Most people feel a combination of feelings, and these feelings change from day to day and week to week. Keep in mind as you lead this meeting that feelings are not good or bad, they just are. Model supportive, non-judgmental responses for the rest of the group.

After the warm-up, list the feelings described in Touchstone Four on the chalkboard or flipchart:

• Shock, Numbness, Denial, Disbelief

• Disorganization, Confusion, Searching, Yearning

• Anxiety, Panic, Fear

• Explosive Emotions

• Guilt, Regret, Self-Blame, Shame, Embarrassment

• Sadness, Depression, Loneliness, Vulnerability

• Relief, Release

• Integration, Reconciliation

You can then jump into a general discussion in which group members share the feelings they've had as part of their grief experience.

Another way to broach this discussion would be to give each group member a small sticky-note tablet and have them write down the feelings they've had, one per page. Then have them stick the sticky notes up and down their sleeves. You're having your group "wear their hearts on their sleeves!" That's a good thing, because it's a metaphor for healthy mourning (expressing your grief outside yourself)!

This can lead to a discussion that not only affirms the normalcy and naturalness of each of these feelings, but also encourages group members to EXPRESS these feelings in some way—to not only grieve, but to mourn.

Finally, try to save the second half of this meeting for open discussion.

Important: Touchstone Four covers clinical depression. Even though you may not be a trained or licensed therapist, as group leader it is your responsibility to help identify group members who may be in need of additional help. If this discussion reveals signs of clinical depression or suicidal thoughts, wait until the end of the group meeting and ask to talk individually to the depressed group member. Talk to him or her about your concerns and offer to help link him or her with extra help. Then follow up outside of class!

Homework

For the next meeting, each participant should be asked to read Touchstone Five— Recognize You Are Not Crazy (pp. 113-138) and complete the companion journal section (pp. 81-92).

Session Five Notes

_____

_____

_____

_____

_____

_____

_____

_____

_____

Support group meeting plan—Session Six

Touchstone Five—Recognize You Are Not Crazy

Am I crazy? This is such a common question in grief that many mourners ask it of themselves. So, this is a very important area to explore in your support group. Many people will be relieved to learn they are normal. Mutual support often evolves from this valuable discussion.

Write down the "going crazy" experiences outlined in Touchstone Five. Put them up on the chalkboard or flipchart.

- Sudden Changes in Mood
- Memory Lapses and Time Distortion
- Polyphasic Behavior and Thinking Challenges
- Psychic Numbing, Disorientation, Disconnection
- Self-Focus or Feeling Selfish
- Rethinking and Restorative Retelling of the Story
- Powerlessness and Helplessness
- Loss of Energy and Lethargy of Grief
- A Feeling of Before the Suicide and After the Suicide
- Expressing Feelings More Openly Than in the Past
- Grief and Loss Overload
- Griefbursts, Pangs, or Spasms
- Crying and Sobbing
- Borrowed Tears
- Linking Objects and Memorabilia
- Carried Grief from Other Losses
- Suicidal Thoughts
- Dreams and Nightmares
- Anniversary and Holiday Grief Occasions
- Ritual-Stimulated Reactions, Seasonal Reactions, Music-Stimulated Reactions, and Age-Correspondence Reactions

This Touchstone, like many of the others, could spur a discussion that could last for hours. You must use your discretion about where to take this discussion. Your group members may also teach you where the discussion should lead. Be flexible and attentive to their needs above all.

Important: Touchstones Five covers the topic of suicidal thoughts. It is appropriate for you to devote a few minutes of this meeting to a discussion of suicidal thoughts. You might ask: Has anyone here had suicidal thoughts since the death? Tell us about them. Helping group members distinguish between normal, passive thoughts of one's own death and active suicidal plans may also be appropriate. Even though you may not be a trained or licensed therapist, as group leader it is your responsibility to help identify group members who may be in need of additional help. If this discussion reveals signs of active suicidal thoughts, wait until the end of the group meeting and ask to talk individually to the affected group member. Talk to him or her about your concerns and offer to help link him or her with extra help. Then follow up outside of class!

Homework

For the next meeting, each participant should be asked to read Touchstone Six – Understanding the Six Needs of Mourning (pp. 139-154) and complete the companion journal (pp. 93-110).

Session Six Notes

_____

_____

_____

_____

_____

_____

_____

Support group meeting plan—Session Seven

Touchstone Six—Understanding the Six Needs of Mourning

Try starting this meeting by writing the six central needs of mourning on a chalkboard or flipchart. Each member can refer to the list as he or she talks about these central needs with the group.

The Six Needs of Mourning

1. Accept the reality of the death.

2. Let yourself feel the pain of the loss.

3. Remember the person who died.

4. Develop a new self-identity.

5. Search for meaning.

6. Let others help you—now and always.

The journal questions for Touchstone Six may help participants teach each other about how they are working on these needs. Again, invite but don't force anyone to talk. The other participants will listen and learn.

Some questions you might ask could be:

• Does one of these needs feel most prominent in your grief right now?

• Are you struggling with one of these needs more than the others?

• How is your self-identity changing as a result of the death?

• What "why?" questions do you have about the death? (Field responses and write them on the board.)

• How are you accepting support from others?

If, after the group has had the opportunity to talk about the six central needs of mourning, one or more of the six needs has not been talked about, you may bring them up. Pay particular attention to the sixth need: to let others help you—now and always. Discussion about this need can once again emphasize that healing in grief is a process, not an event. Even after this group concludes, members will need continued support in working on these needs.

It is also a good idea for you as group leader to reiterate and emphasize the concept of "dosing" yourself with the six needs of mourning. They are not needs that you can work on one at a time and complete, checking them off your list. They will invite you to revisit them from time to time.

Remember to leave about half of the group time for open-ended discussion.

Homework

For the next meeting, each participant should be asked to read Touchstone Seven—Nurture Yourself (pp. 155-178) and complete the companion journal (pp. 111-124). Also ask each group member to jot down one self-care tip—one they actually use themselves and that works for them—and bring it to the next meeting. They'll be asked to share their tip with everyone during Session Eight.

Session Seven Notes

_____

_____

_____

_____

_____

_____

_____

_____

_____

_____

Support group meeting plan—Session Eight

Touchstone Seven—Nurture Yourself

Try opening this meeting with a presentation of the self-care tips brought by the group members. One by one, go around the room and have people present their self-care tip and how it has helped them during their grief journeys.

As group facilitator, one of your tasks is to emphasize how important good self-care is during this naturally difficult time. Good self-care, in all of the five realms mentioned in this chapter, lays the foundation for any healing to occur. For example, if you're not taking care of yourself physically, it's easy to see how your physical complaints (illness, pain, etc.) could distract you from your spiritual self-care. Or if you're not meeting your social needs, you're probably not getting the necessary outside support. This Touchstone is an important one because without it, all the others will fail.

Next, write the Five Realms of Nurturing Yourself across the chalkboard or on separate pages on the flip chart:

Physical   Emotional   Cognitive   Social   Spiritual

Divide your group members into five smaller groups and assign each group one of the Five Realms. Ask each group to come up with a list of doable, practical ways that they could nurture themselves in their assigned realm. The litmus test for an idea to make the list is the question: Would I actually try this? If the answer is yes, put your idea on the list. If the answer is... well, probably not...don't put it on the list. The lists should also include ideas group members themselves have actually used and benefited from.

After each small group has had 20 minutes or so to generate their lists, have them present them to the group at large. Add ideas that other group participants vocalize during this presentation. (You might consider collecting all the tips generated tonight and then typing them up to distribute to the group at the next meeting.)

21

Additional discussion points can come from the journal questions for Touchstone Seven.

Some question you might ask could be:

- How is your body responding to the stress you are experiencing?
- What gives you pleasure and joy in your life?
- What do you feel gratitude for in your life right now?
- Have your friendships or your social circle changed since the death?
- How do you nurture your spirit?

Use the remainder of the meeting for open-ended discussion and sharing.

Homework

For the next meeting, each participant should be asked to read Touchstone Eight—Reach Out for Help (pp.179-195) and complete the companion journal section (pp. 125-132).

Session Eight Notes

_____

_____

_____

_____

_____

_____

_____

_____

_____

_____

_____

_____

_____

Support group meeting plan—Session Nine

Touchstone Eight—Reach Out for Help

Congratulate group members on being part of a grief support group. By coming to group meetings and sharing their thoughts and feelings with others, they are helping themselves achieve Touchstone Eight—reaching out for help.

Ask: Whom do you turn to for help? This discussion, in addition to the journaling they have already done on this topic, can help group members see that there are a number of people in their lives they can rely on for love and support. Sometimes group members just need a little encouragement accessing that support—opening up to the people who love them and being more forthcoming about their needs.

The "Rule of Thirds" (*Understanding Your Suicide Grief*, p. 185) is another good topic of conversation for this group meeting. The rule of thirds says that about one-third of the people in your life turn out to be good helpers, one-third are neutral, and the final third are toxic to the journey to healing. This is a good time and place for your group members to vent about this last third of the people in their lives! Encourage them to tell stories about how others have made them feel bad, judged them in negative ways, said hurtful things, etc. Then, counter this discussion with some exploration about the one-third who are the good helpers.

Note that this chapter also contains information on determining if you need professional help. It's appropriate for you to bring up this topic during group discussion; it gives members who are having a particularly difficult time an opportunity to consider whether they might need the additional support of a professional counselor.

Ask group members if they personally relate to any of this information. If they see themselves as needing professional help, offer to talk with them after class and help them decide if grief counseling might benefit them. Remind members that getting help is not a sign of weakness. Indeed, it is a sign of great strength.

Use the remainder of the meeting for open-ended discussion and sharing.

Finally, this chapter discusses the role of grief support groups. Here you are in a (I hope) thriving, healing group. By now the group dynamic should be strong and loyal. If you feel confident that your group is working well, a good closing activity might be to ask group members how they feel about the group and how it is helping them. If you think you might get more candid responses from an anonymous opportunity to talk about the group, pass out blank sheets of paper and ask each group member to write down one or two or three things about how he or she has found the group to be helpful. Give them five minutes to write, then collect the papers and you as leader can read them aloud.

Homework

For the next meeting, participants should be asked to read Touchstone Nine—Seek Integration, Not Resolution (pp. 197-206) and complete the companion journal section (pp. 133-138).

Session Nine Notes

_____

_____

_____

_____

_____

_____

_____

_____

_____

_____

_____

_____

Support group meeting plan—Session Ten

Touchstone Nine—Seek Integration, Not Resolution

This is the meeting in which you review the concept of integration and reconciliation of grief. I say that people don't "get over" or "resolve" their grief, instead they learn to integrate it into their lives. In other words, they learn to accommodate the loss as part of who they are and proceed in their lives with meaning, purpose, and happiness.

You might begin with an open-ended discussion of where people see themselves in the healing process. Then, walk down through the listed signs of reconciliation (p. 201) and see what discussion follows.

Key topics for discussion:

• Ask members what reflections they have about the concept of "reconciliation" versus "recovery" in grief.

• Create an open-ended discussion about hope, faith, and trust in God.

• If the group would be accepting of this discussion, ask about members' beliefs about life after death and the possibility of reunion with the person who took his or her own life.

This chapter also explores the role of hope in healing. The main text tells you that living with hope is living in anticipation of a good that is yet to be. The journal asks journalers if they have hope for their healing. How is hope playing a role in the experience of group members at this time? Lead a discussion about hope and its presence (or absence) in the hearts of group members today.

Use the remainder of the meeting for open-ended discussion and sharing.

Homework

For the next meeting, participants should be asked to read Touchstone Ten—Appreciate Your Transformation (pp. 207-215) and complete the companion journal section (pp. 139-144).

Session Ten Notes

_____

_____

_____

_____

_____

_____

_____

_____

_____

_____

_____

_____

_____

_____

_____

_____

_____

_____

_____

_____

_____

_____

_____

_____

Support group meeting plan—Session Eleven

Touchstone Ten—Appreciate Your Transformation

The journey through grief is life-changing. When you leave the wilderness of your grief, you are simply not the same person you were when you entered the wilderness.

How are you changing as a result of this death? This is the topic of session eleven.

Some questions you might ask the group at this meeting include:

- How is your day-to-day life changing?

- How are your spiritual beliefs changing?

- How are your relationships with others changing?

- How are your values changing?

- What new attitudes, insights, and skills have you discovered?

Don't forget to remind group members that while suicide grief does often result in growth, it is not growth we masochistically go looking for. The death is not "justified" by the growth group members may describe. (You may want to spend a few minutes talking as a group about how everyone feels about the price they had to pay for this growth.)

You might write down the different "Growth Means…" for everyone to see on the board or a flipchart. Invite people to express which of these they can most relate to and believe are becoming part of their life experience.

This chapter also reviews the concept of purpose in life. Ask your group if they believe they have a purpose in life and if so, to please share it with the group. This will often lead to interesting and heartfelt discussions about goals for the future—which is an important topic for your group to review at this point. (After all, you only have one meeting left!) Given this opportunity, group members will often encourage one another in their intentions

27

to do something about their newfound (or newly strengthened) purposes in life.

Use the remainder of the meeting for open-ended discussion and sharing.

Keep in mind you should be helping members prepare to graduate from the group. This is your next-to-last meeting, and you will want to be conscious of the need to prepare the group for leave-taking.

Homework

Group members have already completed reading *Understanding Your Suicide Grief* and filling out the companion journal. So there is no homework per se this week. You might consider if there is an activity you would like them to do in the coming week. (For example, you could ask group members to write a generic letter to new support group members. The next time you run a group, you could read these letters of encouragement and support as ice breakers at your first session.) It might also be a good idea to ask everyone to bring a special snack for the next meeting, since it is kind of a bon voyage party.

Do ask members to reflect on what the group experience has been like for them. You will commonly see some expressions of resistance to the reality that the group will end next week. Use your facilitator skills to help the group openly acknowledge any thoughts and feelings related to this reluctance.

Session Eleven Notes

_____

_____

_____

_____

_____

28

Support group meeting plan—Session Twelve

Graduation

Graduation—it's always a bittersweet occasion. It's a time of ending as well as a time of new beginnings. For your grief support group members, it's a time to say thank you and goodbye, and re-emerge into their lives.

It's appropriate to remind your group that just because the support group is ending, it does NOT mean that their life transition is. And their need to continue to receive support from others certainly does not end after this final session. Be conscious of helping members identify additional sources of support in your community. Other members may need to talk out their plans to graduate to an open-ended support group or individual counseling.

This meeting is also about graduation. Encourage each member to express what he or she feels was gained from this group experience. You may consider having each participant give a verbal gift to a fellow participant. This is a positive comment a member has observed about a fellow member during the support group. Each person is encouraged, but not forced, to participate in this verbal gift-giving.

As part of the graduation, you may also want to give certificates of support group completion to each member. (See p. 46 for a sample certificate. Feel free to creatively amend it to suit your needs.) Share food and drink and openly discuss whatever is on your group's minds and hearts.

Group members who want to stay in touch can be encouraged to share their phone numbers or e-mail addresses with others. If this hasn't already happened (it often does earlier in the group's natural cycle), you can take charge of this role by asking those who want to to write their names, phone numbers, and e-mail addresses on a piece of paper you'll pass around. After the meeting you'll photocopy the list and send it to everyone who signed up.

Conclude this meeting by thanking everyone for attending the support group, and reinforce that you hope each member has been helped in his or her healing journey.

Pat yourself on the back. You have just completed a successful suicide grief support group!

Session Twelve Notes

_____

_____

_____

_____

_____

_____

_____

_____

_____

_____

_____

_____

_____

_____

_____

_____

_____

_____

_____

_____

_____

_____

_____

_____

_____

_____

_____

_____

_____

_____

Appendix A: The support group's developmental phases

Why is it important to understand that support groups go through developmental phases? Because knowledge of these phases allows you to both respect and nurture the natural unfolding of the group's development. For example, if you were to expect in-depth self-evaluation of all members at the first meeting, you would not be respecting the reality that this kind of sharing generally does not happen until group trust has been established over time.

Groups tend to develop in a cyclical manner. This means that grief integration needs such as "the telling of the story" tend to be met again and again but at progressively deeper levels of meaning. Of course, individual group members have a vital influence on the process of group development; therefore the outline that follows is very theoretical.

Phase One: Warm-up and establishing of group purpose and limits

In the beginning of a support group, you can anticipate some normal anxiety about the general uncertainty of "what will happen here." Group members may be questioning their capacity to tolerate their own and others' pain. So, be aware that many group members will attend with a certain amount of hesitancy and some questions about whether or not they should even be here.

Among the questions that may go through their minds during this phase: Who else is in this group? How do their losses relate to mine? Will they understand me or judge me? Will I feel comfortable with these people? What will we talk about? Are there certain expectations the group will have of me? Will the leader make it "safe" for me to just be who I am? Will I have to talk, even if at times I don't want to? Can I trust these people?

Behaviorally, members will tend to reflect their unique personalities. Some will be more expressive, while others may be silent and withdrawn. This initial period of getting to know each other is critical for what will or will not follow.

The leader plays a critical role in making it safe during this initial phase of the group's development. Here the primary leadership roles include:

* clarifying the purpose of the group.
* gently encouraging each member to "tell his or her story."
* assisting in the creation of ground rules for the group.
* modeling listening and helping everyone feel as if they belong here.
* facilitating details such as time of meetings, formats, etc.

Phase Two: Tentative self-disclosure and exploring group boundaries

This is the phase where members begin to learn what is expected to happen in the group. Every group has expectations (spoken or unspoken) about what will happen in the group meeting. Essentially, members are learning how to be participating members of the support group.

At this stage members begin to see themselves as a group and disclose more about themselves. Often this self-disclosure is rather tentative. It's as if the group is exploring whether it is safe to move to a deeper level of risk.

Differences in interpersonal styles and ways of coping with loss become more apparent during this phase, particularly among those members who are more independent and "take charge"-oriented with their grief journeys. Ann the Advice-Giver, Albert the Academic and Molly the Missing (see pp. 38-43) may begin to display their behavioral ways of relating to the group.

Through increasing self-disclosure and the exploring of group norms or boundaries, members begin to learn more about each other, the leader, and themselves. During this phase the primary leadership roles include:

- continuing to model listening, openness and caring.
- continuing to clarify member expectations of the group.
- reminding members of the ground rules established at the first meeting.
- providing a group format and facilitating any activities or homework to be discussed.
- being responsive to conflicts and problems that might evolve.

Phase Three: In-depth self-exploration and encountering the pain of grief

As the group grows and develops, a subtle but important movement takes place. The group begins to move away from the initial discovery of the "why" of the group and toward an increasing involvement in the work of mourning the loss of the people who took their own lives. At this phase, the group has shifted from second to third gear and is beginning to develop group trust at a deeper level. A natural insider/outsider feeling often begins to develop and certain members may begin to express how important the group is to them. Now the group is feeling good about itself and members look forward to each meeting.

Informal co-leaders may begin to emerge; try not to let this pose a threat to the group or the designated leader (you!) A higher rate of interpersonal self-disclosure and in-depth self-expression is now taking place. Interactions between members become more intense and emotional.

At this point, you as leader may have to become more supportively confrontive with problem members who try to detour the group from its primary purposes. Also during this phase, group members may begin to work more actively on helping themselves and others learn new ways of embracing their losses.

Leadership roles during this phase include:

* continuing to model listening, openness, and caring.
* being supportive of continued participation of group members.
* assisting the group in dealing with any conflicts and problems that might evolve.
* making appropriate adjustments to content and format for improvement of the group.
* allowing and encouraging the group to be more self-responsible.

Phase Four: Commitment to continued healing and growth

During this phase, many members begin to ask for and reach out to others for mutual help and support. The group ambiance takes on a more relaxed tone. Members feel safe and "at home" in the group.

While you should not withdraw as leader, you should be able to share more and more responsibility with group members. You will notice group members modeling empathetic caring responses and trying to crystallize for the group new insights into the grief journey.

Remember—not every group meeting will go smoothly. You will have good meetings, great meetings, some not-so-good meetings, and maybe even some bad meetings. Try using humor to acknowledge a bad meeting.

Phase Four is clearly the most valuable phase in the life of the grief support group. In some ways, if the prior phases have been reached, it's like the group is on autopilot. Earlier concerns and developmental phases have been achieved and the group is moving at a faster pace. Respect and trust levels are way up, which allows members to share what they need to share.

At this phase, the group process is typified by much more open-ended expression of thoughts and feelings. Activities you have planned may need to be eliminated as the group seems to need more time for open discussion. By this time members are genuinely concerned about the well-being of other members. Any missing members become a focus of discussion. Participants will want to know, "Why isn't Mary here tonight?"

Members also openly share their own encounters with suicide grief during this phase. Participants take a more active role in their own healing and talk of how the group has helped them see themselves in an honest way. Group members will also often express their feelings of closeness to other members during this phase. In sum, the group's members have discovered their individual, personal suicide loss journeys—thanks in large part to the interdependence of the group experience.

Primary leadership roles during this phase include:

- continuing to model listening, openness, and caring.

- being supportive of continued participation of group members.

- modeling of shared leadership principles.

- assisting the group in dealing with any conflicts and problems that might arise.

- making appropriate adjustments to content and format as the group evolves.

Phase Five: Preparation for and leaving the group

Obviously, the grief support group that progresses through the above four phases of development creates support and assists members in ways frequently lacking in our mourning-avoiding culture. Also obvious is that the kind of intimacy developed in the support group environment creates natural problems of separation when the group must come to an end.

Careful attention must be paid to the importance of this ending. After all, the group's closure is another loss for the group's members. Many grief support groups are so successful they resist ending. However, "graduation" from the support group is an important step toward integration of the suicide experience into their lives.

Expect a certain amount of ambiguity of feelings about the ending of the group. Ending may elicit withdrawal in some, sadness in others, and happiness in yet others. A theme of general optimism and feelings of progress and healing should override these natural feelings of loss. As group leader, you will need to be sensitive to any and all feelings connected to members leaving the group.

Reflecting on and affirming the growth that has been experienced in the group is a vital part of this phase. One or possibly two meetings should be focused on saying goodbye to each other as a group and supporting hopes for continued healing of the wounds of grief and loss. There will probably be both some tears and some laughter as the group moves toward graduation. Enjoy this and be proud that you have effectively and compassionately led this group toward integration.

Primary leadership roles during this last phase include:

- creating safe opportunities for members to say goodbye to each other and to the group.

- recognizing and understanding the dynamics that occur when a group begins to end.

- encouraging reflection on individual and group growth related to the grief journey.

- providing referral for additional resources to those in need.

- conducting an evaluation of the group.

A reminder: this five-phase, theoretical model will be influenced by the unique personalities of your group members as well as by your own leadership style. Some groups will naturally move more quickly through these phases than others. The most important thing you can do as group leader is to ask yourself how you can make it safe for these phases to evolve. If your group is not moving forward or seems to be stuck, try to discern why the members don't feel a sense of trust or safety.

Appendix B: Responding to problems in the group

Murphy's Law ensures that no grief support group will run smoothly 100 percent of the time. Problems will arise, typically due to one of three reasons:

1. *Lack of leader preparation.* "Where are we supposed to meet?" "How long was this meeting supposed to last?" "I thought *you* were going to bring the name tags!" If administrative details aren't properly taken care of, group members will feel left in the lurch. On the other hand, problems can also arise when a leader is too controlling. In general, a lack of effective leadership skills can result in a number of negative consequences. Proper support group facilitator training will help you circumvent these problems.

2. *Discrepancies between group members' expectations and leaders' expectations.* Each individual group member will have his or her own expectations for the group. The place to vocalize these various expectations is in your pre-screening process and during the drafting of the group ground rules. Without clarifying mutual expectations, the group is set up for failure.

3. *Individual participant problems.* Each person brings a unique personality and history to the group. No matter how well you pre-screen members, you will encounter challenging participants who will test your skills as a group leader. Effective intervention in these cases requires that you first establish a caring, trusting relationship between you and each group member. Sometimes group members will themselves intervene by confronting each other about problems arising in the group.

Following are descriptions of some of the more common challenging folks you're likely to encounter in your groups. I've suggested ways you might deal with each of them, but do keep in mind that confronting an individual member in front of the rest of the group is rarely a good idea. Instead, ask to meet with him or her individually after the meeting. And remember, even when you must confront, lead with your heart and with compassion. Usually, problem members are just teaching you about their personalities and their unique ways of interacting with others.

Amy the Absent

Amy is the group member who is there, but is not there. Sometimes this person is still in the initial shock wave from the death and is simply unable to speak. Amy may have tried to attend the support group too early in her grief journey, or she may just need the group to be patient and understanding. However, there are also Amys who consciously choose not to participate and interact with the group in passive-aggressive ways: "I'm here, but I don't plan to be a part of this group."

Appropriate ways to intervene: From the very first session on, make an effort to help everyone feel involved and a part of the group. Create safe ways to invite the Amys in, such as asking, "Amy, I'm wondering what your week has been like since we met last?" Making eye contact even when this person is quiet is also a way of engaging her and inviting her participation. If your Amy is an outright passive-aggressive, you may need to talk to her individually and explore whether the group can appropriately meet her needs at this time. You may discover that some people are just very shy, quiet, or overwhelmed—yet they perceive they are getting a lot out of the group experience. If you can sometimes help them let the group know this, the group can often embrace and accept them for the quiet people they are.

Ann the Advice-Giver

Even though you have created a ground rule that says, "Do not give advice unless it is asked for," you will, no doubt, have an Ann in one of your groups sometime. Ann is quick to inform others what they should do to solve problems. She may try to "take over" under the guise of being helpful.

Appropriate ways to intervene: Gently remind Ann of the ground rule about advice-giving or ask, "Did you feel that John needed you to tell him what to do about his concerns?" Obviously, the goal is to prevent advice-giving in your group unless it is asked for.

Albert the Academic

Albert is the intellectual in the group and often likes to show off his huge knowledge base. He might quote a recent article he read or expose a little-known theory to explain his, or more likely someone else's, behavior. Analysis and interpretation are Albert's joys in life! There may be a condescending quality to his tone; generally he thinks he knows more than most anyone else in the group.

Appropriate ways to intervene: Initially, I often allow Albert's natural defense mechanism to help him ease into the group. However, when it becomes a consistent pattern, it can be destructive to the group. Therefore, I sometimes try saying things like, "Albert, you have really helped us understand what the articles say, but sometimes I wonder how you *feel*." Of course, he may lack insight, but it is worth a try. Sometimes when I know my relationship with Albert is strong I'll say, "Albert, I know that I sometimes have a tendency to intellectualize things that are painful for me. I wonder if you see that same tendency in yourself?"

Bob the Blamer

Bob is the participant who projects that other group members (or, other people in general) are the ones who cause his problems. This self-defeating thought pattern has often been a part of his coping mechanisms for some time. Bobs often projects an accompanying sense that no one has ever understood him and no one ever will. This self-crippling stance wears thin very quickly with members who are trying to honestly look at themselves and sort out new directions in their lives.

Appropriate ways to intervene: Compassionately attempt to help Bob become more self-responsible and eliminate the tendency to blame. Well-timed, tentative comments like, "Bob, sometimes I'm struck by how often you find fault with others. I'm wondering what would happen for you if you looked inside yourself at times instead of outside?" A supportive confrontation like this has the potential of getting Bob more connected to himself and help him make positive changes.

Charlene the Challenging

Charlene is the participant who likes to challenge the leader. She might accuse you of not knowing what you are doing, which in turn may cause you to question yourself. Charlene likes to put you on the spot and tries to make you look incompetent in the eyes of the group. Her challenges are more often made in front of the group instead of privately.

Appropriate ways to intervene: Be certain you don't get defensive when the challenges come forth. This would be just what Charlene wants and would probably lead to more challenges. It is often appropriate to acknowledge her comment, but then offer to meet her after the group to better understand each other. While you may be tempted to initiate a dialogue that will prove your competence, resist the urge. The group will most often respect your decision to deflect the criticism and discuss the situation individually with Charlene.

Fred the Forced

Fred is the group member who is there because someone else wants him there. He has no intention of participating and feels he is being forced by a friend or family member. He hopes everyone will forget he is present and will leave him alone. Fred rarely makes eye contact with anyone, particularly the group leader. If questioned or invited to participate, he often passes and looks put upon.

Appropriate ways to intervene: Try to screen this person out in your pre-screening process because this person will be counterproductive if not outright damaging to the group. Once Fred is in the group, you can attempt to make him feel welcome and warmly invite his participation. However, if that doesn't work, the group will be well-served if you meet with Fred individually and explore the possibility of him leaving the group. You may also consider referring Fred to individual counseling, but he will usually resist this suggestion.

Holly the Holy Roller

Holly spends so much time talking about heaven that people wonder if her feet are on the ground! While faith values are very important and should be explored, the Hollys of the group often alienate other members by quoting scripture. Holly usually projects a lack of any personal problems and may perceive other members' pain as a "lack of faith."

Appropriate ways to intervene: Support that what works for one person may not work for another. You can accept how important Holly's faith is to her while also (with appropriate timing and pacing) helping her and the group acknowledge that having faith and mourning are not mutually exclusive. If Holly is advice-giving about the need for everyone to have faith like hers, you must gently remind her of the ground rules and redirect the group in ways supportive to everyone present.

Ivan the Interrupter

Ivan is the group member who, consciously or unconsciously, is always interrupting other people. He can't seem to keep his mouth shut. Other participants will begin to see it coming and will start hesitating to share for fear they will be interrupted. Ivan must be helped to control his interrupting tendencies or he will destroy the very heart of the group.

Appropriate ways to intervene: Gently remind Ivan of the "equal time" ground rule. When this fails, go to the next step: "Ivan, I notice that sometimes you have a tendency to interrupt the person who is talking. Are you aware of this?" You can then offer to help him when he does interrupt; it can often be done in good humor with excellent results.

Paul the Preacher

Paul has a lot in common with Holly, but he often preaches about anything and everything. The group experience provides Paul with an audience. He may attempt to dominate the group as he tells the group what they should and should not do. He is usually very well-intentioned, but tends to wear thin with the group. He may seem overly rehearsed, as if he has preached his message many times.

Appropriate ways to intervene: Gently remind Paul of the "equal time" ground rule, as well as the "advice-giving" ground rule. You might express how his tendency to preach impacts *you*. Say, for example, "Sometimes when I listen to you, Paul, I wonder if you really want to hear what others think and feel." Again, this confrontation must be well-timed and intended to help him reflect on how he is impacting the group.

Ralph the Rambler

Ralph is a close cousin of Paul the Preacher — he just changes subjects more often. Ralph tends to bore the group as he rambles on, yet seems to say little of substance related to the needs of the group. He rarely completes his sentences in ways that allow others to talk; he just keeps running on and on and on. The group kind of lets out a silent groan as soon as Ralph utters his first words. Without a doubt, one rambling Ralph can ruin your group if you don't effectively intervene.

Appropriate ways to intervene: Once again, return to the ground rules related to "equal time." If this fails, step up your efforts to help Ralph by being supportively direct about his tendency to talk a lot. The group will often be able to help if you ask them if anyone was able to follow what Ralph just said. There is some risk in this approach in that a fellow group member may attack Ralph for rambling on all the time and saying little. Again, if all else fails, ask to speak with Ralph after the meeting and attempt to compassionately help him look at his rambling and become a more controlled contributor to the group.

Sarah the Socializer

Sarah's goal is to keep the group from getting too serious about anything. The problem here, of course, is that death by suicide will naturally bring about serious, thoughtful, painful discussions. Sarah may see the group as an opportunity to be with other people and socialize in a fun way. Obviously, her expectations are different than the group's. Sarah may laugh when everyone else is sad or make inappropriate comments to distract the group from the work at hand.

Appropriate ways to intervene: First, understand that many people protect themselves from getting hurt by trying to stay in a social mode or be humorous. Try well-timed, sensitive comments like, "I notice that sometimes you laugh when others are sad. How do you understand that about yourself?" Or, "When I see you laugh like that, I wonder what you are feeling?" Some Sarahs will lack insight into their use of socializing while others will appreciate your efforts to help them.

Wally the We-Sayer

Wally attempts to talk for everyone in the group or to be the group spokesperson. "We think we should . . ." is a common lead for this person. Wally assumes (and this is what creates problems) that everyone thinks and feels the same as he does. Allowing the "we" messages to continue often causes quieter members to give in to the "we talk" Wally espouses. Resentment can grow and some members will probably drop out and not even tell you why.

Appropriate ways to intervene: Ask Wally if he is speaking for every person in the group or ask the group if there is anyone who doesn't agree with Wally's statement. If it is healthy, your group will provide a safe atmosphere for people to express their unique personalities. Gently confronting Wally often helps achieve that goal.

**Red Flags Suggesting Referral
for Individual Counseling**

There are some grieving people whose needs will be met more effectively in individual counseling or therapy. The following "red flags" should alert you to the need for making an appropriate referral.

• Persistent thoughts of suicide, expressions of serious suicide intent, or the development of a specific suicide plan

• Arriving at your group under the influence of alcohol or drugs

• Previous diagnosis of a serious mental health disorder

• Profound symptoms of anxiety or depression that interfere with the ability to do basic self-care

• Uncontrollable rage directed at others

• Physical harm to self or others

• Uncontrollable phobias, such as an inability to be by themselves at any time

• Characteristics of mourning (such as anger or guilt) that do not appear to change or soften at all over a period of months

Note: the above list is not all-inclusive. You should use your good judgment as to whether or not a group member would benefit more from individual counseling than from a support group. It is also important for you as a group leader to realize that, even when you make a referral for individual counseling, the person may choose not to take your advice.

A Final Word to Suicide Grief Support Group Leaders

With appropriate preparation and a compassionate heart, you can and will help many people through the wilderness of the grief experience in your support groups. Facilitating grief groups not only transforms members, it transforms leaders. Remember to honor your own continued transformation. You have likely grown in your own wisdom, your own understanding, and your own compassion. I thank you for leading these support groups and wish you the very best!

Certificate of Support Group Completion

Be it known that on this day, _____ has completed
the Understanding Your Suicide Grief Support Group and has immersed himself or herself in the
ten essential Touchstones for finding hope and healing his or her heart:

Touchstone One—Open to the Presence of Your Loss
Touchstone Two—Dispel the Misconceptions about Suicide and Grief and Mourning
Touchstone Three—Embrace the Uniqueness of Your Suicide Grief
Touchstone Four—Explore Your Feelings of Loss
Touchstone Five—Recognize You Are Not Crazy
Touchstone Six—Understand the Six Needs of Mourning
Touchstone Seven—Nurture Yourself
Touchstone Eight—Reach Out for Help
Touchstone Nine—Seek Integration—Not Resolution
Touchstone Ten—Appreciate Your Transformation

You have given and received support from fellow group members. Your presence and sharing of your experience with
suicide grief have touched the lives of many, and for that we are grateful. We wish you continued healing and hope
for a renewed purposefulness and happiness in life.

_____
Group Facilitator

_____
Date

This support group model is based on the work of Dr. Alan D. Wolfelt as outlined in his book *Understanding Your Suicide Grief*, www.centerforloss.com

Suicide Support Group Leader Self-Evaluation Form

Please take a few minutes to record your thoughts and feelings about leading this support group. You may either fill out this form on this page of the book, or you may photocopy the blank form.

How did you feel in leading this group?

_____

_____

_____

_____

_____

_____

_____

What were some of your initial impressions of the group? How did your impressions change over the course of the 12 meetings?

_____

_____

_____

_____

_____

_____

_____

_____

_____

Which member did you have more difficulty with than others? Why?

_____

_____

_____

_____

_____

_____

How did you work with this member, and what was the outcome?

_____

_____

_____

_____

What did you learn from this group?

_____

_____

_____

_____

_____

_____

_____

_____

What changes will you make for future groups you lead?

_____

_____

_____

_____

_____

_____

_____

_____

_____

_____

_____

What additional training might you benefit from?

_____

_____

_____

_____

_____

_____

_____

_____

_____

_____

_____

_____

Support Group Member Evaluation Form

Please take a few minutes to record your thoughts and feelings about participating in this support group.

What impact has this group experience had on your grief journey?

_____

_____

_____

_____

_____

_____

_____

_____

_____

_____

_____

_____

What were the most valuable aspects of this group experience for you?

_____

_____

_____

_____

_____

_____

_____

_____

_____

_____

_____

_____

What did you learn about yourself and your grief journey?

_____

_____

_____

_____

_____

_____

_____

_____

What changes have you seen or experienced in yourself that may be due, in part, to the support group experience?

_____

_____

_____

_____

_____

_____

_____

What are some of your perceptions of the group leader(s) and their style of leadership?

_____

_____

_____

_____

_____

What would you recommend to improve this support group?

_____

_____

_____

_____

_____

_____

_____

_____

_____

_____

If you could describe in a few sentences what this group has meant to you, what would you say?

_____

_____

_____

_____

_____

_____

_____

_____

_____

_____

_____

To contact Dr. Wolfelt and for more information on his books and workshops, please write, call, or e-mail:

Dr. Alan Wolfelt
Center for Loss and Life Transition
3735 Broken Bow Road
Fort Collins, CO 80526
(970) 226-6050
www.centerforloss.com
DrWolfelt@centerforloss.com

Understanding Your Suicide Grief

When someone loved takes his or her own life, the naturally complex and painful grief that follows is typically overwhelming. The circumstances of the death were traumatic, and the resulting grief for survivors is also traumatic. This compassionate resource explores the unique responses inherent to suicide grief.

Using the metaphor of the wilderness, Dr. Wolfelt introduces ten Touchstones that will assist the survivor in what is often a complicated grief journey. Learning to identify and rely on the Touchstones helps those touched by suicide find their way to hope and healing.

ISBN 978-1-879651-58-6 • 194 pages • softcover • $14.95

The Understanding Your Suicide Grief Journal

Exploring the Ten Essential Touchstones

For many people, journaling is an excellent way to process their many painful thoughts and feelings after a death. While private and independent, journaling is still the outward expression of grief. And is is through the outward expression of grief that we heal.

ISBN 978-1-879651-59-3 • 136 pages • softcover • $14.95

The Wilderness of Suicide Grief

Finding Your Way

A beautiful, hardcover gift book version of *Understanding Your Suicide Grief*

This excerpted version of *Understanding Your Suicide Grief* makes an excellent gift for anyone grieving the suicide death of someone loved. This is an ideal book for the bedside or coffee table. Pick it up before bed and read just a few pages. You'll be carried off to sleep by its gentle, affirming messages of hope and healing.

ISBN 978-1-879651-68-5 • hardcover • 128 pages • $15.95

Living in the Shadow of the Ghosts of Grief
Step into the Light

Reconcile old losses and open the door to infinite joy and love

Are you depressed? Anxious? Angry? Do you have trouble with trust and intimacy? Do you feel a lack of meaning and purpose in your life? You may well be *Living in the Shadow of the Ghosts of Grief*.

When you suffer a loss of any kind—whether through abuse, divorce, job loss, the death of someone loved or other transitions, you naturally grieve inside. To heal your grief, you must express it. That is, you must mourn your grief. If you don't, you will carry your grief into your future, and it will undermine your happiness for the rest of your life.

This compassionate guide will help you learn to identify and mourn your carried grief so you can go on to live the joyful, whole life you deserve.

ISBN 978-1-879651-51-7 • 160 pages • softcover • $13.95